The Hero

The Hero

Hélène Sanguinetti

translated by Ann Cefola

chax 2018

Library of Congress Cataloging-in-Publication Data

Names: Sanguinetti, Helene, 1951- author. | Cefola, Ann, translator.
Title: The hero / Helene Sanguinetti ; translated by Ann Cefola.
Description: [Tucson, Arizona] : Chax Press, 2018.
Identifiers: LCCN 2018016922 | ISBN 9781946104144 (pbk.)
Classification: LCC PQ2719.A57 A2 2018 | DDC 841/.92--dc23
LC record available at https://lccn.loc.gov/2018016922

The original of this work, in French, was published in France by Flammarion in 2008. We are grateful to the editor and publisher of that book for permission to publish the current translation. No portion of this book, its cover image, or the book in its entirety, may be reprinted without previous explicit permission from the author and translator.

Grateful acknowledgment is made to the editors of the following journals who published sections of *The Hero: Asymptote, The Dirty Goat, eleven eleven, em: a review of text and image, Exchanges, The International Poetry Review, Inventory,* and *St. Petersburg Review.*

Chax Press books are supported by gifts from individual donors.
Please see *https://chax.org/support/* for more information.

For Alain

"After the bridge underwater, after stones, this is how far I will go in midst of life, in this state driving and calling mules."

"If the current wants me, if the stones want me," that's what he adds this instant, Caterpillar goes where great Will goes, thus.

Then, leaving hands and legs to claws under grass: "If I am
singer and storyteller, pebbles that pull the skin of my feet, will swallow
my tongue"

Because, always: the cripple.

Cruel men, who are you to be more than you're able, And standing on the cart
his profile – brows' curve – his cheekbones – attract sun that
passes on this world, And this cruel world breathes, leaves its apron on the nail,
a braid on its shoulder, leaves to rain and die

BAH!

WE'LL BE

OLD.

VERY

OLD.

VERY

BAD

BACKS

NONSTOP

REPEATING

THE SAME THINGS—

WITHOUT

TEETH

WHAT BREAD

A FROZEN GLOVE

FOR THE FOREHEAD

IN ORDER

TO STAY

YET

A LITTLE

Cloud fathers who unwind from sky, Come here too I'm so small that there's no room except for cotton and stuttering!

Powerless: caterpillar passes away, Man, its cut head between his hands

Nonstop prayers in my eyes, twigs, moss, drops,
dust particles, thus collected and best given back to this earth of which I
am, I surrender

And so it was. Before even Going, before even Putting its fingers lightly
on his temple, love love that does and says: Beloved, And the blood necessary,
from bread, from basil, a handful of gleaming olives

And says: there. Left in the dish, back again, those newborn. And then the
tears necessary for this always, *because who comes back if he comes back,*
aglancebehindtheshoulderwoodfloorshiningtothewallstothosestuck
unstuckanailcut a, shoulder cut a, lone heron, *oh flowers on the
table of dear recommendations*

In the street, she, who walks next to him, young friend so handsome, And both dressed
in white, eyes also leap long-legged far as the sky under the
pines it's evening, and wind

If we're taking part, the hut will be quickly pitched, and solid, that we'll make in the shelter of the rock, the shape of our heart, the night damp with wolves,

When I was much smaller than small, Yog of Ice – Yog of Fire, this is whence he came, far from a hero, like today, at the head of a leaf pile in the clearing, pushed by wind they'd been pushed, there they are

And so it is. Born with his eyes, his nose, his mouth, his ears, his sex, he says: "Truly, I am complete."

(The heart was in the trees, hardly a nest)

Much much later a small craft came from the back of the landscape came
behind reeds, softly you oars and walking sticks on two
riverbanks, which murmur, we see, all glide to find the traveler so
thoughtful on the bank,
"Let's be ready."

He is ready. He put aside his cardboard valise, big stone of weariness
in a paper journal: he leaves a world worn, by beggars, by ink
stains

That's what he thinks.
Then trembles without thought, sparrow-like, or like a barefoot in the
desert burning from its insides, and She-Earth ⸻
"Friend of mine, my all and all, where are we going, where?"

I brush against you, I walk at your pace, and if I waddle along, it's sky plus sun
hung on the tip of your white blouse, from the tip of your turned up sleeve,
We are far-and-forgotten, with-hard-Fingers-with-black-Fingers, like
we're on the avenue,

she brushes against him, and under the great pine, more than a storm, more than all!
Crows, carry the nightmare far away!

Suddenly, Something from the night, the most obscure cold, Silence so quickly back despite the joy!

Blazing, thin face————*When I was much smaller than small*

Very thin body too, (finer than the smile of death)

Balcony, Kitchen, up there what wind what wind, the pane is
full of black winter summer red swallows, I was king, fountain purveyor,
builder of African Pavilions, Imprisoned, shot despite his
tears. I was a cat, one day, it rained I loved the rain

Butterfly he had been – otherwise where else did the feather that stayed
come from? – above the dead water
of a watering can, from a birdbath in a town garden in time
of peace,

COME IN! COME IN! And he greets the immense crowd gathered, and the horses with
steaming torsos, with steaming nostrils, My Immense My
Empty My Beasts, he clasps them, his eyes rolling to the sky he says to
them really incredible words, The Hero!

FAREWELL! FAREWELL! now. Because he's going away.

And this was the ocean and pine forest endless trunk that dreams with the wind, only one
bird on a very high branch speaking with his
neck,

And passing from his entire body in this place of feathers and sky, the Hero!
for the first time so alone, or really, so far from his mouth left over there on
the edge, Only bird, only immense space of Air and sap

A Big Ape for guide! if he means me, the softer his look will be
Tomorrow that awaits, and with moon I pierce my ear, with moon I go
forgotten, up high where sister stars all alone hastily run, in
my sandals I leave sand, leave, LEAVE. Because it's sea foam
that reached up to here, with earth moss serving as its back, and
soaking it during its nap!

Long needles will enter my book, Not odor! nor fingers, nor
smoke, nor sudden showers from this full summer storm!

Soldier, you roll a cigarette between two fallen bodies the tongue holds
the paper upright, Euxin Sea in the sky, rambling red Ant
crosses, you think about what on the road?

*(Not a book like before! From infinite space gallop and cry with
its beast within born for nothing)*

Ferns return and Fears come, barefoot since the law that has
red eyes, and still wonders

Hence, for you

     (It sleeps, sh!)

*It's been found! What? the little knife. So yes, I carve your name, everywhere, yes, and I
shape shreek! in one stroke, I would also light the fire but how, with one tinder? – in the pocket where it was.
That's to say how much I dream while working, hands to the storm outside,
feet squashing slugs and other little life forms like us, ground level, I
do not dream I hope
     This note more gull than you believe more famished more red: 3 points – 3 horns –
1 face
But nothing of that here, nothing living new,*

And the story which said:
At the top of the swell, mother and father lay down a baby in tears. Then
the other law that wills: that the wave descends, calms the child, makes him sleep and
withdraws to the bottom, leaving a great blue calm all day
(We hear some part spoken and played, and laugh.)

To go far away, taking small steps without stopping, to come closer, find
nothing, to let come, Here's a beautiful place for visitors, and full of a
hospitable aroma, with fig leaves, big vine of crushed palms and cookies
in the bread box. Because we opened the buffet, it's dark, what
was hidden there moves inside the bottom of the sugar bowl,

Then we stuff the valises once more, *ah, dear homeland, how long was
that absence! That I might see you again,*

and the dribbles.
To descend the river, go live in the town near gold and time.
He lay his hips on the sand, the Hero, a heavy dying wasp stuck
on his leg, night stayed in day – *Me too, I stay against you*
and I listen, The dog who barks who smells and The dog who wants to eat

(What'd be sweet would be the arrival of some sort of Fay and her favors!)

Because always, who loves us?

Some girl crosses the place without seeing it, Sun in a corner, what time would it be, you come I forget the poor world, it's a day in the day, some dirt in the light wind, tumbles down

a dog's behind, something
nothing.

Much much later he hesitates between the sea – that he sees from there entirely –
and the mountain behind him the sky, A bear there had written his name with a star, A
pine cried FIRE – HAVE PITY —— *what is there still to learn, let's see,*
since I am amongst rooftops, viaducts? And who will take off these ropes
that keep me from walking?

And so it was, will be, without reason. One slip, several deaths, ladder steps.
Mouth open under the rubble, enough?
Throat of darkness, enough?
Bass voice, foam, enough?

Gentleness asks the hero, sometimes, Since he asks! Gentleness far
from the caves. A carcass came back stinking the blue day
of winter, to little dwarves dumbfounded, swollen, him, their son

*"I am pinned down I have a face!" that's what he cried at the time, making a stain
where he lived*

*And then: "If the summit disappears behind, if life climbs higher than
the mist in its turn missing",*

*Invariably.
"Thanks to the Queen who permits all that."
"And thanks to the King, with his old beard of 77 centuries!"——because
always: the frantic*

I am nailed, oh, my foes and oh, my friends, it is so great, night!
I will be, far, grass that shines and steams, the animal's stubborn gesture, a tip
of my son's ear, and here's the story that will remain, I stay with it on the
shelf between their arms

He draws back then sits trembling on a walk before the black station,
the Hero!
He misses his little house, he misses the sound of water in the tank.
The girl waits for her bus, humming on a fingernail——————he
would open her heart,

Now there's the battle its long claws dug well into their backs the
young girls,

There are Birds so no one falls, no one believes enemies twisted lines
in the bucket bottom, greedy lines that fight, hope and the sky turns
to evening, three drops from above come below and dead water awakens,

Patient opens his arms, lord, lord-closed-eyes
Lord-black-hands-hidden

Call call for help, oh, trees! oh, frogs on the edge and that
swell quiet with the moon, bare-chested, much too late much too night,
greedy night I'm coming already

It's up to me now right away he said, and I'm coming

"May you be on two knees May you be bathed in sweat on the path May you be in tears May you be
Exhausted, Renewed"

He hurried his two swallows' hands hold the last evening at the front,
thus, so that this might be more flight than the caves' child prisoner, the
wells in the cave in the sky a look a couple saved from time,

There, A bridge elsewhere one trembling stride cuts the town in two,
one ran one fled, from *bridges it's like steps, they join, they*
separate, A battle, oh, soldier! comes here to start, rapes, deaths,
cries, help, rupture, burning, betrayal, sacrifice, medals, citations,
betrayal, burning, rupture, help, cries, death, rapes, citations,
medals, sacrifice, all battle the world over

Winning it back,

three reeds rustle under the wind, sorry, He is hot he can put his jacket there, scorching summer is back, who are those there in the photo overexposed outline of a man far away, bends, rangers planted near the young girl, he marries her, her blonde hair,

In leaving, This one, didn't turn around, taken by traffic, all hours intense on the bridge and then the purse that pulls on her shoulder, days before,

The man fades until he disappears at the end of the bridge

The headquarters opened on a row of
courtyards, and doors, a closed down Ivy college, perhaps
an old hospital, priory? A waiting room jam-packed with
men of all ages, all places, all languages.
He sat where he could and he recalled the vacuum of fever, it
stuck. A little old man folded up a sort of beggar's pouch in
blue cloth who hadn't even lifted his head when he had come in,
burst out laughing and greeted him: "Mister, these are the
circumstances that make a man or unmake him!" The voice was
very strange from the body which it left. So young, and so beautiful
really that Daniel who was not especially attentive,
was surprised by it.

She adored the fragrance of his fingers,
she called him Petie, they played tea party, with guests!

An explosion, big stinking drop, rang out suddenly and
shook the panes. Everyone down! cried a leader, only the old man
with the beautiful voice stayed sitting, he pulled out a piece of
champagne cookie from his bag and nibbled throughout the alarm.

She brought a bouquet of zucchini
blossoms to her grandmother Rosemary, but
she was deaf,
or she was not there,
or really dead,
too bad!

The alarm ended, we tried to make the donkeys leave one by one,
poor animals were crushed against the door and shat each one
more than the other, one local looked for a son voluntarily
enlisted, had to absolutely get in, why the donkeys and
not her? She was fat and sweaty, she had jewels on her
ears on her fingers around her neck what fervor!
and then she was too agitated, she wanted to see her son her
little one, who left the house hit on his head because, etc.
The leader arrived reestablishing some sense of order by a long
whistle-blow which hurt everyone's ears. He calmly read a list of
names on a sheet, with addresses, professions, distinguishing
marks, favorite occupation, each Designee signed and a
very young girl smiling with a beautiful blond braid added herself.

If I meet the wolf, I will not speak to him
but I will take his eyes and his teeth,
in order to have a handsome child.

A burst of pigeons crossed the sky on the left. We
left the very narrow straw mattresses which still smelled
of the cave's dampness where they had spent winter, piled up, and
aligned them to lose the least space possible. We
needed to have a chance to fall upon good neighbors or
have a wall against which we could turn over. Daniel
thought suddenly about his wife at the other end of the bridge.

—Please, one more
moment to pray high on the
mountain that you see from here,
and she threw herself
at the feet of the monster
with the blue hair,
she would have moved a rock to pity
with her tears and
fresh breasts palpitating
but the god had
a heart harder than a rock.

NATALINA. – My love left this morning for war.
My love left this morning for war, with a fever.
(She is in the kitchen, sitting, cup in hand. Or she
smokes. In shirt or pajamas or almost nothing) Across the street, they
fight, if I were to go and stand on the balcony, I would be able to see them,
my God! There had been nothing but the bridge to cross "Don't worry,
my dearest, I will come back as fast as I can."
Yesterday, they pointed to a young woman, she had blown a
blowgun pfff! pfff! the round note climbed up to the
window on the other side of the street, despite the trucks which

didn't stop circling, a boy came, he looked, he
blew a flying kiss, below. The girl laughed open-
mouthed, to swallow the kiss, and then she shouted in her
two hands, "I loooooooovvvvvveeeyouuuu, I will come back tomorrow,
be braaaaaaavvvvvveeeeee!"

—*Now, come down, cried the enormous voice*
—*But it's the summer rain, I am slipping on the rock piles, my*
ankles hurt

What she would've done just to be able to touch there, the small face
surrounded by wire mesh? Me I have arms
of a butterfly, it's empty. The evening, just before night, it's
much heavier than night. It's made of a terrible weight,
which goes across, pillages, scrapes, silent, heavy-light-heavy,
evening falls, day lifts, the words are right sometimes.
Who am I speaking to? Who is there?
(She listens, making a big effort to seize something
in the silence of the house)

Or he will climb up high, and will find the lost lamb, peeping
and will Tie it
to the post, its neck so tender,

From here, we hear nothing. No. A little rumbling with
bell-shaped wings, deep under the impact. This isn't the peace
in us, not the peace between us, across the street battle between them
and us. But this-is-not-the-peace still holds the roof over my head
here, three turns of the bolt close the door and outside stays
outside, despite feeling turned upside down within. (She wedges
a lock of hair behind her ear) I would like not to leave sky
of eyes, I would like to drive my eyes into this height and
this roundness, to crumble myself, melt myself there,

Waits for her brothers,
waves her handkerchief so that she can
she has
a back full of smoke
The god works enraged and whimpers, he
is going to climb, h-e c-l-i-m-b-s r-i-g-h-t n-o-w
a king listens to the door
of his horse-drawn coach Girl is naked

at the riverside concert
of water and crickets, everywhere
down in the fields
the poor lift their heads
Going the harvesters are going
Bell ringers of months
hunters of magpie

What can we do, despite good intentions, the rage that we have! And what will be left of my fiancée? more nothing, nothing of nothing. When leaving, he did not turn back, "My dearest, you know, I am not for you nor the future." He faded faded until disappearing at the end of the bridge. He did not turn back, a hero doesn't turn back, he has swollen feet because in every sense he travels the earth, and that the mountains, the streams enter his socks, the oceans too, in the bag on his shoulder he carries his thought, he moves a block of cement, sometimes, he puts it down but too light an animal he feels unwell and takes it back very quickly, he takes it back.

I know it I believe it because your love
is immense, -------------
--------- hungry the hero he climbs on
the roof of the house,
on his homecoming his wife washes his knees,
collects the water that she drinks, oh, Crazy Woman,
who
are you?

I closed the window again and I suddenly realized: he's forgotten everything! That's what I wish for myself, how I wish it! He has no more than a package of cookies. *(At the coatrack, she takes down a huge jacket that she slips on)* Powder, clover and anger, and the weight of a hippopotamus skin, I suppose... *(she laughs)* A cold shell.

(She opens the cupboard) The pastries, made of slow sugars, that's to say they do not rush, they take the time of sugar, they arrive by barge via the Mississippi!

And cheese, a banana, I wait for tomorrow.

Love takes
all the credit ---------- Offer me,
prince, a kiss
found all in the fields,
savage would Carry me away, ----- The prince
will not come so Love sighs
Undoes her eyes
--------------- Tomorrow
the handsome sun

"After the days the years, after, this is where I will want to be
powerless, in this female condition, dog delouser.

Dogs mothers days," and she says wiping her mouth with her
sleeve

But leaving tears and sheets in a bedroom corner, That one:
"I will have a Daughter in my fist, what I am I will have, so people can throw
rocks at me or pull off my feet"

Because, always: to exist.

But others on the steppe, or high in the tower, on the steps, in the corner
by the fire, against the pane, harp on, believe, get quiet, torment an
old man who resting one stork-like leg gets their thoughts all mixed up

Hero, where are you, unless you can be it, not favoring them,
abandoning them, And standing on a silver shield, or really straight behind the cart,
blood-soaked lacerated by the patrol, A sun that paled
which bleeds on the sea it too, The women cut your tresses, they cradle
them in the hollow of an apron!

Poor ones.
They grow, grow more, sunflowers, with their seeds, even the
calmer wood Even eaten by the hungry blue bee for its nest! And
the world rolls up without getting lost,

Pearled breasts
Cut breasts
Holy
Poor!

*Do you believe that inclined to such a discovery we might be still more beautiful
one day their adored, Or taking the fountain's-weary-air, keep
maternity's-finally-full softness, or Tigress about to break free?*

The night lifted your head then your elbow, a standing wick that
sleep would have erected, I fall in your arms like I fall in the dark
street corner dark street specially for this

and when he looks at her, this way, catching her beneath the trees

The night lifted,

You become the prince again, or sultan with eyes — the horse climbed in the
clouds, me carried away clasped above fields, sea,
below shines perhaps all the more as all precious gems, treasures
amassed given as dowry, and there a small boat with motor and
smoke, pushes the day carries it far farewell

11:57 p.m. before the riverbank, for him she left before everyone, the others their
gear, she waits for him, it rains on the avenue cicadas of drops come
down their legs, if you do not come, to die! who else but the moon, anger
love last night,

"But I am not the one who keeps the almond tip, lover between
my teeth" Anger on the pavement, in the stomach and shoulders, travels the real
storm: flashes thunder, lightning, Jupiter's panoply,

Not married at all to his canvas she says, nevertheless that one's fingertip
always lights the lamp, Hero, that one who gives twenty
crickets of kisses on your neck, bites inside

And behind the pane This One, who waits for the body of oil eyes sunny muscles, *Who else more muscles, more fingers*, SILENCE AT LAST SILENCE

or never more will he Sit here,

nor Eat nor Drink on the oilcloth,

nor Send smoke in curls up to the ceiling

Climbs scaffolding, Sun, Boy, a commentary of sparks, then
another star's pain, what, pain! the earth climbs the soft slope
it was a hill, getting lost in conversation,

and who will follow the night's debris with feet, on the path, pebbles pools with
feet so well aimed, carved?

Ostrich leans over, and wire mesh leans over, Great Hero is thirsty, he blows, recalls
a tip of obscure sky, a yellow ochre, a troop of bandits with pointed and yellow
teeth, they lions He leader bige shos bbbig laaaugh and
hands holding stomach to keep from falling laughing so hard

that all the stolen pennies

may roll in the ditch with thorns

The girlfriend's bed is unmade, it is unmade for a dream, it Takes Off,
Scent of soup doesn't prevent the Boyfriend from carrying it far, there are steps heard
crunching, Overcoat which smells winter,

Soon winter soon a head a kiss, on him, shining bird on
top of the cypress it's there now where He lives

Because here's how night was shattered:

Joyous Voice said she is no more

BAH!

FAMINE

WILL BE

HEART

FACE

WILL BE

SINCE

FACE

WILL BE

MORE

THAN PU-

LLED

PAINLESS

EYELESS

TEETH OF

THE DEAD

SING

SING

SING

SING

And Girl who said,
I am what I am, braids woodcutter's blood no shame in my apron no
worn brakes nor explosives in my socks,

said,
purer pain than hers, stone harder and whiter on the tongue
than hers?

Was saying,
I am beautiful in the pools! chase the golden pigeon! its wings stuffed
with love! it sings the Farmer's return! Rich! Doesn't squint anymore! Exactly!

Frantic retreat under blue sky, glassful of blue sky, Descending she flies
she shouts herself hoarse, and pebbles ricochet as far as the gutter, under the sky. Thus
passes each Sunday: never Dirty never Balking never
Forgetting! And the trees murmur inspired by such unrivalled beauty, spy
trees

Living trees that have faraway feet, and under the moss a scent of
cavalrymen, who believe in riding when the sun gets its strength back than rats
swarming the river, And crying under your soles, drunk ladies, ladies
spread on the grass,

Since at the time nothing was there,

since the storm suddenly burst, a pig disguised as god, from his leg
pulling Beautiful chubby-cheeked hope, a drop stayed on the back of
a hazel leaf, a tuft,

he stops with His Best Sweetheart, under the tree, she clasps the heavy head in
her legs,

Victory of a landscape

Victory of a thorn

Victory of a sigh

Am beautiful in the pools! chase the golden pigeon! stuff the love story
in its wings, Farmer returned, Rich, doesn't squint anymore, Exactly

The women have the truth and truth since, really, always, their names Rose,
Fire and pureblood Calamity, Louise, Little Curl, Gracious,
Jenny – empress, Infinity, Emma, Martha with the revolver, Polly,
A Cruel One, Jeanne and Madeleine nee Perpetual Crush, a face behind the
curtain vanishes with the wind,

pirate women,
knitters,
beheaded

(The people cry and sing, spit clinging to the chest full of holes, lakes)

Spring!

Citizens!

Beggars!

Friends!

Daughters!

And again primavera their hair, roll in the flowerbed, and sun and trumpets more moronic than the willow

Ah, our very nearest and dearest standing follow You, Succeed you

While withdrawing, it falls to her to clasp a match given each one, the women were so small on the edge, empty on the edge, running away and red from swearing evasively, *follow You, Announce you*

True too: many, very young dead of cold under the snow, and among the living, Three shrews and their magic, three furies, fourteen kind ones, six wicked, thirty-eight traitors with nothing, the lazy, we count them again we recount we await the latest reports, who will come?

Because who will come

here, now, the path which brings a cart here comes but the horse
stays under the shade of the same tree and prefers flies which buzz
above, below, rather than hearing the complaints regrets of a woman a little crazy!

Under the same tree, well, lives a horse, also a man who was
living, he braided white roses so high that no one living
could smell their heart so high

or a cloud where an intangible inhabitant leans over, As it was
always will be

Little one, come back inside and don't forget your basket in the woods

Lift your leg and lift your knee, higher! Hero looks like the wolf
we adore, his profile, beetle is cold from thinking he comes and the cortege of
suitors he Sits a moment in the clearing

"She loved him!"

"She loved me!"

The hero let his heart his fist fall again on the floor again
on the floor at his feet, a flight of brothers, a jackal

Count and recount his fragments under a porch, this in a stream of air
it's night youth far behind the shop window shines a box a key a
general's hat a shaved neck

And it's over
True: Engaged, he was, scarcely believing in such happiness,

He goes up high from the side, sees the village, the smoke and his valise
he puts anywhere in his hurry to see it all again, where is she where is
she where are, August-burning-killing-blood half-exploded-blood-up
to-teeth he falls and it's over

There's a fly and here are eyes

The Hero brushes the dust off his sleeve, swerves his neck to the
rising sun, And here is the well: rendezvous with a little stammerer in
well-fitted shoes and cantankerous, an ape's friend

Or rendezvous in a hut, three drunk men, villains and
idiots laying down, Or a street corner, a movie house, as far as the station
steps before they're torn down

What to do if this one loves the wells, and climbs there so much he loves the stars the old
bones surfacing from debris, *we ate seal meat here,*
Species of angels and hair linked here at least once

What do I still see with eyes given me and with hands
I seize what, whatever I can: flecks, crystals, Ears make what of
this cry that bounces on the rocks, what is this animal's cry ⎯⎯⎯⎯

⎯⎯⎯⎯⎯⎯to cross the doorstep and greet the head of the missing

He had this phrase on board a donkey

"He has the hand of a donkey,"

(gentle approach of a Youth who believes he will eat)

a hazelnut of air shines in this hand,

a horror of being dead

Then no matter what really you say to yourself in this broken down language
full of potholes, and there were people with head, arms and legs————
hands went in the soft flour, eggs, milk and mint
to keep house,

A man enters. His jacket turned inside out, he travels.
Hello, and hello————————————so among nothing to arrive before the little
door, she is in wood, thick black, snow and tar argue over the
poor mouth pinned mouth, poor violet face

(face deposited so, only a very minute feather breathes)

Between a nameless man who wears an iron ring around his neck and who
smiles, and inclines his head to nod graciously tender in his curled
hair he sweats he came far, his sweater is so dirty it's almost
gray, his nails are dirty

*Hello and Hello, sit down head of the Plum Trees, and you head of the Rose Bushes, and
you head of the Water Lilies, and you hello and hello, head of the Door and of nothing,*

It's an unknown country, many waiting on steps, they have
tears or they sing, nursing infants right on their knees, they are beyond
light white clothes, sandy moon on their eyes

What do I hear do I hear once, What do the flowers
say to each other over there and what really are they all thinking

And so it is: now shoemakers run all over the countryside with their
dogs, careful on the canvas with your rubber boots! no
trespassing, they trespass, scoundrels, nothing they can't do! now put down
the pitchforks in this corner an eternal star

breathless hearts of dogs rise again, exhausted, rise again little leaves,
claws grip advance and horns also leave for the raid, a
Hero walks into Hell,

an Eyelid greets his own silent snuggled against the door of the cave, the handsome face stayed high the Painted Goddess guards it, via fledglings under the clouds

to See nothing better

to love then die better

to become shadow and eat shadow better

(Be brave nothing leaves for nothing!)

Oh, she doesn't complain, and even covered with fat for a long
time fled, *I walk since I walk looking at you,* Without his knowing
without result she still says something, in his velvet ear

And so it was. Even before Meeting again. Even before Reopening, Setting the head
down, pillow on the silver dish she says: this makes the room smell dead the forgotten
and I descend the steps, I am going downstairs, then the horse makes a noise
in its neck, shakes off white drool, what age and what age you, you have changed
you're better,

Oh good, if possible so late! 5 p.m. high near a cloud the great lakes call,
lizard Somersaults, wind gusts, leaves blow off, cries of slaughter,
rrrrrrrrrrrrrrrrrrrrrrrrrrrrr, an enraged bulldog demolishes a gate, in the hero's
ears and eyes live this whirlwind, this unlikely
life

All the books dead on the shelves and to be dead they fall, on
bits of gravel, the Little Sister she swallows the dust there this day, she
pulls out the small bottle, hill, pickaxe all near since one guards them
in their eyes the rough hand, one guards them from stones and stones

It was their territory with reason, (and all leaving great joy with
dances), the mountain the sea sorrowless they are, a toothless
smile that makes the mouth round the old kiss arrives on their cheeks in
tears the circle weeps, sun returns from sun goes away

At the time where I was, Head of nothing was I, like yesterday and tomorrow

A poor man returns to the edge of the stairs, a practical joke recaptures him poorer still, thin voice and handsome clothes, prince's nails, from castles with terraces on the still poorer sea, with worn out shoes, a bit of vengeance, *oh my friend so handsome*

At the time when I was there, I endured cold hunger, This silk,
Girl! this golden hair, this is all madness

And so it is. Even a bandit trembles, swears twisted with love so strong that he pulls out bedroom bars, he bleeds on the sheets, in the morning his blood still flows on the grass, *without you my black soul goes away into nothingness, Princess, my princess,* How he exasperates the beautiful Dawn, he exasperates her,

The beautiful exasperated Dawn
        She does her hair (sitting) before the pane that the buses rattle she
guesses who will love and not come, across the street it's Annette, female butterfly
on the balcony, her breasts overflowing, this one, *really, kill her or hang me!*

Above the skylight there are caskets, flowers, jars of makeup, a
ballroom dress and gleaming baton to provide cadence to
rowers,

This man left the tip of the earth to gain a lot, she waits for him in this
world, *from my throat I leave One phrase shining and hanging,*

Here's the evening again and here's the same moon seen from here yesterday and wind,
Venus, shining Daughter, reappeared

This day of plague,

....

A brave man took to the sea to wage war, red hair, Red,
healthy color.

And If he returns, he will be great, swinging as he walks, he will have a big
hooked nose, back turned around under the bridge, never cold, Eroe will be his destiny

Red hero!
White the line waiting!
Green the homecoming cheers!

Wait, for the photo, it snaps. Rain from yesterday evening, violin rain,
very cold. Since it existed it will exist, the way one puts quarters
in a pocket, one puts twigs Going to bed, Rising (the scatterbrained,
the thoughtful).

Black for the bees' silence as soon as it snows and no one!

Walking away from the port,

having aged,

from rosebushes over there

in big strides

between two fingers: ants, blood of ants,

and on the trunk: a steady stream climbs descends

The grocery is still open?

it's always open!
it's a young Arab.

even Sunday! but

last Tuesday

it was closed, the little sister got married
she quit the store, she's happy

The stabbed run, hide themselves, buy pullovers in a shop window where they
are, "Who comes in hears the clock, this day of plague"

You three, die.

In his nose he has medicine, and garlic, paper rubbed with
snot, from an idle ape's ass! There's one that carves a craggy cloud
and whips a goat, Gored from above (another recovered by the Cloud
of love)

And rain streams on the iron, the face rain glides

Breast opens
Canal doesn't have

Here's a Bald man then a Redhead, they bow, On the well rim drop
squashes then drop squashes

This isn't a well, a fabulously rich silence

A request for wine
Other throws it

Eroe, Air, water

And once upon a time a she-ass with very white skin, who carried the black earth trotting along, the trees accompanied her in their way, greening again despite the ends of the world. Some cicadas, and kinds of crickets still there, a glass of water stayed there too. Humans, few in number, hid in caves, the lower body, arms, hindered by veils bought for centuries at low prices. Some had given or sold their tongue to science, others had tossed it roadside, a train platform, some put it out to dry, pinned on an invisible clothesline so that from faraway you could believe, with the breeze, a memory of a seagull. If someone could've seen her, he would have been astonished by the whiteness of this animal, of her solitude all the same so incomprehensible, was she really the last of her species? With her stubborn refusal to move, a legendary stubbornness certainly but never proven in such extreme conditions.

Red the hero!

One day, she stopped under the noon sun and sweating, worn out, she spoke to it a long time. How to understand what she said to it?
Another day, she drank in a canal which started to flow again mysteriously under her tongue, what did the water of this canal

become then, how to know? The she-ass turned with the earth, or really perhaps was it, her four hooves shining, that made the globe turn round. She was going. At last, (this at the end of a very stifling afternoon) she came to a height where there had been an opulent town on the south-west coast of Africa. Two dogs were sleeping in the dust.

One, particularly old or ailing, lifted its head and tried to open its swollen eyes. The other, much younger or a little crazy, and doubtless happy to see someone, jumped on her paws yapping like never before. Better than a good-natured royal, and tender, the she-ass, far from kicking or biting, laughed with the dog neighing a little sound. And gazing at each other, walked together as far as the sea.

Red the hero!
White the line waiting!

There was a very pure and blonde sand which bore their curious games of hide-and-seek and their unlikely exchange of themed jokes. For hours. It was so fine this sand and so soft that without consulting one another the two new friends decided to spend the night there, under several faraway stars which did not shine unless the wind returned in a gust.

The night stayed black but the she-ass's coat so intensely white was enough to give light and the dog seemed totally reassured by its glow.

The infinite sound of waves calmed them. Then it was the populated silence of sleep, on the shore the sea rolled.

And that, the strange companionship, lasted a long time, undoubtedly for years.

One evening, one very old evening, the dog was designated to die or he died suddenly, that's to say that he felt in all his body an immense weight that held him immobile on the tar of the road and finally made him close his eyes forever. And the little body – little in relationship to all that surrounded it, so big the countryside – sunk in a block and came back immediately in the slim pocket of himself which shrunk almost from eyesight. (The dog had come in again).

White the line waiting!
Green the homecoming cheers!

The she-ass once again found her old solitude, that before the dog, after the canal, another end of the world. She had aged perhaps, how to know with such an animal? How to tell if her fur had whitened, she who was so white? Had it tarnished? Her step was really still lively, finally the same. Her eyes: immense and tender lashes, like before.

The road was straight and a little winding. Below, in the valley, a great agitation reigned, because there were men again or really shapes that strongly resembled them. The animal was considerably astonished by them, she who had not met whoever may be in such a long time.

FORWARD! FORWARD! As if the command could come from the mountain above, or the far horizon, the sea with its waves powerful and soft, that is to say, from oneself, from inside, the loins ready to bite. Her hooves ricocheted on the iced tar, because it was suddenly very cold, and even something of a fine layer of frost covered the countryside. In her descent, she slipped and had a hard time taking the last bend which opened on a space immense and flat: deserted. Where then had gone those that she had seen? And what silence! Where to stop to lay down a little, sleep a little? A cabin appeared from which rose smoke straight into the pale sky. The animal, suddenly happy, approached it.

Green the homecoming cheers!
Black for the silence of bees
as soon as it snows and no one!

This was not a cabin but a kind of box without any visible exit, forming a lid, laid down on the ground. The smoke nevertheless escaped above, from nowhere. An indescribable sadness came from there. The white she-ass butted her head and again butted her head, furiously, to shake the whole as if to pop a cork. Impossible. This was harder and heavier than a cast-iron block.

Black for the silence of bees
as soon as it snows and no one!

She trembled, covered all over by a very very great fatigue, against which there was nothing to do. The air absorbed all of her, diluting her whiteness in a sky turned gray. Or snow, in dense flakes? She did not have a second's hesitation, closed her splendid eyes. Tiny, cold, silent, she had found her place again between the bear and the giraffe at the bottom of a valise for pygmies, on a storage shelf.

This day that stinks, dislocates.

In the shop window, it stays for whoever-looks-will hope, with ends of everything,
Whatever, nicely presented, the hero's cortege with sleigh bells, and
little girl by the hand, her blonde doll too

Feet tangled, turn back on the path, searching night to rest or
Respectfully close the dialogue,

RED, TO THE HERO! A new cry, of the immense chest gathered
on the edge of the wharf and standing on the banks, and old teams old
teeth to pull the ropes, right on the bank on the edge of the wharf,

RED!
Fishes' red sides shining dead between their fingers, Drool and
balderdash still hitched together to this day, Thus,

It was necessary to put to bed someone who didn't have anymore legs

Look at the river

To become holy (in good health)

You climb a wall – smoke rises – rock dug out

We're literally going back to a feudal system: serfs and kings. Or you move

Here's the night.
Good, it's her, she moans, good, she cries x 100

Move where?

Here's the rain with its wings on the train window

For some time he spits out his hands
He waltzes with fashionable worn-out shoes!

That's to say he could barely contain himself between a bowl of coffee and
a dispute

*I want to absorb the most happiness possible, to have it later, it's
stirring*

The boss crushes the employee's head in his hands. White face.

The boss gnaws everything he touches (doesn't eat what he can smell)

*Part of the face licked clean by the moon: far from the hero having a quick dip,
drinking*

*The boss alone stepped forward to break without breaking, but rock sweat, very
far from the sun*

"He doesn't turn the page" beak pinned beak, careful to have shouted hoarse with calm

The boss came then left, called: it's this way (He leaves.)

*Little wandering bits of ice
on the water's surface*

*Umbrella magnolia
Magnolia tripetala*

Athletes come running, sex shining
Joy suffocated under the shower curtain

Possolo! possolo! clouds pass, compare the countrysides
of the world

Pool, Flower
My Dears, what are you doing here?

A warrior had visions, what, the couturier of the big day? and you,
little one, with your bag which weighs tons, Iphigenia, go up to the altar, list
of words seen from the sky

Comfort
  Desireness
    Unpleasantnness

      Disspleasure

        Destiny

         Oroomny

Oroom
  Hope
  To hope
   Joy

        The Thought
        To think it
        Quiet
         Doroom
          Doomskdoroom

     Astonishment

Fake
Stump
Prince

      Loyal desire
      Loyal will
      Loyal heart

  Jubilation
  Tribulation Grateness
     Falsehood

Help

Weakness

Distress
Dead   Princess

Time
Gracelice
Lucklice
Malice

Kindly
Sighs
April
Ah   Summer

Shame
Crazy   Faber   Fiddller

Antiquity   Insanity
You Die

Carlo
Steamboat

It was the history of the canal the canal's poem, nothing, Gestures of
hero born here: heros' bugs, stayed high on the tapestry, sputter
and supper with heads, here this one world (its voices wedged under the door)

Safe journey to its feathers and colors! and to the others who arrive dirty
feathers dragging in the dust and water overflowing gutters,
safe journey

Because always poesia, joy horror

All right! Little Sun and Little-Silk have come back on the lawn glides
the strange spectacle of their love glides a small boat returned it too
an exhausted father with fish, and he comes back in and says to the family in the
house "Heavens! May life be better later on!" all right!

The lamp is lit it breathes, the floor breathes, it's not late,
rain perfumes gutter and windows, and no one is cold,

Last house shelter stands abandoned, after after, with air and ants and
other regular stumbling visitors, It smells of chocolate a kitten thrown out the
window Saved bouncing on the dahlias,

Welcome Life much later
Welcome Inaccessible love
Welcome to the Anger of Tears

Anger and joy leave the vial in the stream! with bubbles for
the unhappy and their bundles on the path, bubbles and bubbles for
Averell Dalton–dreaming pursued by the sheriff

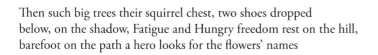

Then such big trees their squirrel chest, two shoes dropped
below, on the shadow, Fatigue and Hungry freedom rest on the hill,
barefoot on the path a hero looks for the flowers' names

a cloud

an iron heron

a girl on horseback

*Where do you come from….., He searches………………., only understands you on tip-toe or in
the corner of the window, And still searches
fists clenched, mercifully the rainy day falls so close to the ocean,
Does not cease to: Think – Hope – Shine better,*

He gives a *kiss of rain*, eats on the ocean shore, he grew old and his
dogs grew old, too much to drown them but loves them still, makes them
go to bed at the foot of a library of rocks, and shining water

She grows old and her sisters grow old,

————how to escape you, Little Torturer with Sugared Lips,
They say and remember: lianas, sisters! And copper! – how
cool the embankment below the Sierra, and to the other Hooked Nose,

poesia-face-violet-hollowed-poisoned, *Another Hunchback behind the window comes in* with a caramel apple so round and red and sweet, *eats the white girl punctured white*

and suddenly Fanfare, the best beribboned bugles?

BAH!
HEARTLESS
WHO NO
LONGER HAS
HANDS
ARE
EATEN
FACE
EATS
HANDS
SINCE
THE GREAT
HUNGER
FIFTY
AND SOME
RED
TO THE
TIP
PITY
FOR ALL
THE FINGERS
RED
TENDER
TO THE
TIP
ALLIES
CRAZY

Hatred of tragedy, always, but the Hero, vulture, helmet, trucker
or bust hailed in the dining room, and mouth more wet than slender
woman in the tent at reveille, Or : unfeminine girl-hero really knocking
and shouting 33 Holy Family Street

crazy girl, frenzied when she found out, *May everything explode a disaster, all the
chimneys, walls, streets, May they burn and me*

TO BE BETRAYED, TO HAVE VAGUELY LOVED

AND OF THE CHILD THAT WAS THERE AND HE CUT IN TWO THERE, ONE FOR
HIS WORK, THE OTHER IN A DREAM ROLLED IN A BALL,

who, to discuss it around the table – it's Christmas at this table,
or let it return to his house even dressed up, even powdered. Send him
to look! little face with ember eyes in the cradle!

Where is his house, where is yours distant Baptist, The girl danced, she
closed her eyes she spoke, she danced, spoke, and spoke, carried the dish,
rose under cheers, how? Such heavy head in the center of that dripping
silver dish,

I'm a divine monarch! Faraway priest on a lagoon! No,
chocolate Buddha! Behind the curtain behind a street with posters of
skin, *you see, there*

And so it was even before we found them dead in the cave, to decode them there
under the sun, driving sea below, and in the shelves where men
shouted and women also shouted, in the sea the lost were all at the
bottom, GOOD-BYE, GOOD-BYE, now, because everyone goes away

Where does he come from exactly, what name, who is his father, and this ring, this
hair, these teeth, seem barbaric to everyone

——TO BE AN EEL, A NAKED STOMACH AND NAKED ARMS,
TURNED AROUND FROM THE FOREHEAD TO THE FEET UNDER THE
TORCHES, LEVEL WITH THE TABLE MOUTHS SALIVA EYES,

——FROM, BETWEEN YOUR LEGS-------AND FROM KISS ON HIGH THE FRUIT
SHAKEN, TO CARRY YOU AWAY BEHIND THE CURTAIN

——TO BE SMALL IN THE ROOM AND ENRAGED BY SERVING OBEYING
DECEIVING TO BE DECEIVED INTO LOVING ME BY HATING YOU

—TO BE HORRIFIED BY A STAR, A HORN THERE, TO HAVE THE
KEYS AT THE WAIST, A STONE BEARD, TO KILL ALL THE
CHILDREN,

—TO PULL OUT THE DANCERS' HANDS THEIR FEET, TO
SHOW IMAGES OF THE DEAD THEY ARE VERY DEAD SLIT THROAT
DECAPITATED

—UNABLE TO SPEAK FROM SWALLOWING PEBBLES FROM DRAGGING ME
BY ROPES VEIN AFTER VEIN *THIS WAS A MOTHER WHO LIVED*
OUTSIDE

——TO EXIT BIG BOXES, EVERYONE FALLING ON FLAGSTONES,
MY SHIRT NOISELESSLY AND THE COLD

——TO BE A HORSE, A SCRATCH, THE MUSCLE THAT TREMBLES AND
SMOKES NEAR ITS TAIL, APPROACHING ME FROM THE FENCE, FROM
BARBED WIRE THIS IS MY CHEST STOPPED, MY EYES IN YOU

——TO ARRIVE BEHIND THE DOOR TO LISTEN BEFORE SEEING
A LETTER WITH FLOWERS A KIND OF LETTER SIGNED
ROGER, YOUR LADY, YOUR BROTHER, ANITA, MISTER TOUZON

102

——TO COME BACK AFTER THE CELEBRATION, TO SWEAR, TO OPEN SHUTTERS TO SEE
DAY

——TO HAVE BIG FINGERS ON THE WOOD FLOOR KNEELING BUT ONE OF HER
KNEES DIVINE KNEECAP POISED ON THE MOSS SOON MORNING
TO RETIE HER SHOE, A CLOUD OF SMOKE

——LEAVES, AND AROMA, SHE PRACTICALLY VENUS AND YOU SLUT
ON A DATE!

——TO RAMBLE ON WITH A CHERRY STONE, THE CHERRY'S SOLITUDE ALSO
AS MANY THINGS AS WE ARE, ROUGH REAL THINGS
BARELY STRAW MATRESSES UNDERWEAR FORGOTTEN ON THE LINE

——TO WISH FOR WIND CAPTAIN TO TWIST THE BOATS ONE HAND OF AN IGNORAMUS,

——TO SAY AT THE WINDOW'S EDGE AND RUNNING AS FAR AS THE
BALCONY "I WANT AND I WANT" THE CRYSTAL LAMP EXPLODES
IN HER ARMS,

—DRIED HEART IN THE PIPE'S FIRE, FROM THE PLAIN WITH
FIRES, OF FIRE AND AIR INHALED WISELY DIGESTED!

—FROM A TUNDRA FACE FAT FACE

—TO PLACE A FOOT THEN ANOTHER UNDER THE MOON LISTENING
WITHOUT THINKING OF PLACING A ROSE THEN TWO WILL OPEN

Phrases rise and thus come from sun and flies all March,
phrases glided closed, hero April returned, getting off a moving train,
three flecks against his collar, all April cold, shot cannon and
shot cannon

Already from the cries, April
This was a dead mother, since there was one, there will be more!

April all from cold,
Ice floe, I think gravely about you, pity fish, ice floe!

This same day dove in the gutter, remained
a task,
a cardboard bear,
a head

And so it was even before, ...
.........................GOOD-BYE, GOOD-BYE, because everyone vanishes

I can no longer burn myself so much, a letter he left, to see Who's coming on the path nothing more comes, or nightmare, cavalcade, barking

After death, a medal is placed on the buffet

After the father's cries, Of course, him again, with arrows in his heels, and no one falls

Weeping a long time we called her, Weeping, woman who twists her
braids, what remained, comb, sweaters, ace bandages, pushed in a travel bag,
glad for it all,

Stayed at the foot of the armchair, tried to count, recount, Needed
light sheets, a little mint, what would come of a phrase pulled out,
like dying and being born at once, a leopard's leap in the
branches,

and always: two grease-smeared fingers in suspenders, bursting cheeks
full of air

*Barren woman (says the ogre) I will eat you and I will start at the bottom,
the object of so much talk*

And always: existence, far, existence
Planted with arrows and dandelions, basin water

Like running, disheveling hair, roaring, there's Joy in such Leaps,
throwing his glove on the meadow, and the mare sends the world clouds
made from her nostrils, whirlwinds

Very soft. A wisp of a kind of sky. Very soft. Perhaps hot.
Friend, she says to herself walking, and her shoulders don't hurt at all bearing the head
of He who comes

Who eats with his fingers, kneeling, Day needs him to eat, a lot, and he still knows nothing, he
bursts out laughing in his sleeve, with his teeth he makes music,

                horses' gold
Rag with gold the hero collected in a square, the police ask for
papers, the rag, the gold, He rolls up his sleeves again spits on his heel,
saves the beetle, from tar

Thus, 4 coins to Each as they were able, spinning around and
around, somewhere else ditto, in silence or crashing, let's imagine a little we look out
the porthole, what do you say captain and your sister who always stammers more
during Revolutions

So runs the song, he runs as he can and everyone runs under a
bridge several where there's no wind, a stomach three times its size if there's wind, the valises closed
then weighed, sky starts again to be born, let's go

Now that I think of it and since the garden flowers and the birds of poetry drink,

It was softness, he held her by the hand her wrist teaching him how
with a bit of tongue and skin harsh and stubborn at last
wordless, Friend forever, she said, why do you want us to forget so
quickly, loved words of love, wanted,

Friend said he, skin suffices

Since the sky started again since softness——————and who speaks
across grass? Called grass even the thread left in the sand without
grumbling is called grass and wind comes wind makes it move

Back home, he's there, he leaves the trail, all dream and disaster one day
then the opposite the next, he leaves on the trail an adventure like
no other

To eat, he sits on striped carpet, a bowl of soup at its center, a moth at the gaslight, spins a
delicate phrase, the bowl
steaming

From words of nothing,

On fingers, that we dare to kiss and kiss again, then in the mouth, then
swallowed, with the thrushes and dates every stone on the ground immense earth
with children come from air, quiet says one, sing says another, and each making a
bouquet,

Stones ring their eyes and the tiny queen's forehead with pearls like
no one else, surrounding her earth is round, round cheeks

(We climb the palm tops better than an ape)

let's ask for news, so we can be gracious hosts, a breath would be
heavier to nurse, *as much messengers as scraps, slivers of
fennel,* a tiny spider exited from there

*What was will be, and who, Hero, what for shadow, what for front wall,
the decadent red paint, Hero since he was and will be I change
my shirt I marry this girl on the balcony with a cat*

So far from the person I once was see-sawing under trees, on the pontoon with
wheels and senseless jumps overshooting (better than an ape) the water and
beyond, I left it on the shore kissed and embraced

There's the Hero in the arms of This woman chosen with shouts, little boys bounce on the
lawn-little girls cry, this day is magnificent,
resplendent with happiness, full sun, *Skin suffices*

So far from the person I once was see-sawing under the trees, on the pontoon,

Now give him something to drink, if he dies cover him with skins, Cry
and cry then come back with spring of butterflies of trout,
Immense sea much farther still and even deeper farther out

SOMEONE, *perched on another's shoulders, in the middle of the crowd* – WE
WO — NNN! I hold the Cup, and I kiss it for everyone on tour of duty,
thank you, thank you my friends…
We won! we won! Thanks, to all the men. All the women. And overwhelming
thanks for the life of each man and woman.

ANOTHER – WE wo-n! we wo-n! we wo-n! Eyes burst
with happiness. And we're not dead, this is good news
for everyone, and for our children far away. Mary, Joseph, thanks.
(pulling away to the camera) My Cecile, I kiss you, your little fat man who
loves you, who adores you! Ever so much.

ANOTHER. – There's a bull in us there's a volcano
in us, we want and want. There is a volcano in us
in those moments, and questions. Questions of
principle that go along with the job. Thanks for not Slipping. Is it the
little one's fault? (One example, cited from memory)

ONE. – Did you kill someone?
Right at the dormer window, at a range of 30 meters, it was more beautiful
than all the words in creation, thanks Cocro, for what started kneeling
and ended kissing the trampled grass.

ANOTHER. – We think differently, battle didn't take the place of
being: letting time pass, enjoying the return to all kinds of sweet things,
this doe or that kitten, depending on what town or really countryside,
everywhere you can find a person Who Grumbles or Who Laughs

She
carried away
her baby on the
plain,
it
comes to him
with big eyes
but
he
does not grow up,
Alouette
alouette
stung
by the sky
show me,
Nothing,
Any
work
never resists
the simplest
despair,
show me where
you may be,
Groaning crying falling

A SOLDIER. – Don't be afraid, we definitely caught them, everyone's under the rubble.

CHIEF WARRANT OFFICER GEORGE, *who struggles violently to go further* – Speed up dammit, I have a real tip, this is the tenth, we're going to win.

ANOTHER. – We're going to act as if we recognize them but we won't recognize any of them.

Daniel – but this is unbelievable, what are you doing here? You're not joking, not you– Was this always your dream? You got married perhaps, to that tall woman?

(Faraway cries) We... wo-n…. We... wo-n… We wo-n...Fucked them up the ass-ass...   Hooray!!!

(Nearby) **We won...fucked them up the ass-ass... Hooray!!!**

Oh
Sinbad,
it's
doing your hair
with
the dawn,
dawn
with dawn's
fingers,
painting
with
her very
soft eyes oh,
Star on the tip of your Babouche

DANIEL. – You know, this type, he opens the fridge, there's
the rest of the meat and green beans, or tuna in tomato
sauce, he takes them out on the table, he's going to eat and when he brings
the fork to his lips, She is all there, missing, a
block of woman missing behind his teeth,

Billy goat
also
after
Goat
Goat
stayed
Billy goat
went
gone back up
droplets
shone
in
its hair

THE OTHER. – To disappear, change life, why not?
Look at the medusas, they're there, then they're not

DANIEL. – I am vanishing. This is well-known: the less one understands,
the more it diminishes a person.
What have you won? A doll, a Donald Duck, a
sausage?

Medusa
searches for
her husband,
on the glacier
she
looks, and her
claws
stick into the
feathers of
those who arrive,
Hero
doesn't leave doesn't
lose
his mind,
licks
the ugly woman,
has a soft
tongue
the nursling
licks
and
cradles
nothing
but
his eyes

DANIEL. – And you are you still in engineering?

THE OTHER. – I went back to Sperm, they have the best
pills on the market, welcome returns, no side effects,
paradise.
But I have a lot of worries about my daughter, the youngest, she
doesn't talk anymore, for three years she's shut herself in her room.
No one understands, I've brought her everywhere, with Louise we don't
know what to do, you remember Louise? She says it's my fault,
that I don't have any patience, but I swear to you, it's she who
has too much, she has too much! 'You're sick, you want a
Gamegirl, you want to stay at home, eat a little, to make me
happy…'
I can't do it anymore,

Looking
straight
within him
and

says it's
your turn let's go to
your turn,
show
everyone
that you
can you are hungry
and him
cradles her
and
makes her sleep
Him
pierces
her ear
Him
takes everything
from Her
= dust
on the road.
The recommended
bones

DANIEL. – Here's Max, my friend Max, about whom I've spoken often. Natalina, my wife. My wife is a girl

from the North, practically a man, she had been extremely
courageous during the recent events. Shall we have a drink?
(A young boy spins around a tray loaded with beer mugs)

NATALINA. – A nonalcohol beer, if possible,
sir?

THE YOUNG BOY. – We're not a pharmacy here!

A MAN, *kneeling before his dog,* — You realize, my Dick,
everyone, we won our bet: we're happy, we can
look, touch sometimes even caress, and with time, all the
stories will be true, and reality will be true too, and
good dogs will make good friends, my Dick,

Beauty
of place

starts
in my heart,
tongue
lagoons
softness
window,
thus
sprinkled
and
hidden
for the best of
night
that
returns I return

ANOTHER. – You talk about a horse! A meteorite, its eyes,
like wings. Or really a cloud descended one
second to make a zouave, to dry the trail. A mist,
a prince of wind. They had run off with everything and you
you come back home, you dry your feet on the doormat thinking
about it, you tidy up your affairs thinking about it, all evening you
think about it, the night. There it is, you have to wait, to have a little

of what in its basket to pass to another day, on the other shore, they

dance. We cuddle we search for a dark corner to cuddle

again,

He
came
to drink at the
fountain
finds
a thin
fiancée who
coughs,
at the fountain
evidently,
and
regrets
taking
her size her
reeds to be
with this
mule
who holds him
tight
at the neck
up to the post!

*"May wind
and the breathing shining
sea be with you!"*

A FEMALE NEIGHBOR. – Go on, small ones, take advantage of your youth, full throttle!........................... We will all finish at the same place, in the hole, my God, let's look at the light, we will soon enough be in darkness!

PHILOMENA. – I should have brought a jacket, it's getting more and more damp, with these crickets

*They
don't have
the right
to go
in
the street,
the children!*

3Guardian
is no longer
Queen
is fallen
------------is broken
There was
a hole
hole
stretched-----------
deepened
Universe
entered
the
hole

The first firecracker, shot from the small boat crashed on the boat, and at water-level, smoke, a dry sound of fuse lit for nothing. The second also had little luck. But the jubilant crowd looked from the riverbanks, waited without impatience for flowers and fountains in the sky. The entire town was there or almost, to celebrate the new nation, the new bridge reconstructed with scraps of the old, the original which had held marvelously, then inevitably cracked.

Let's resume,
what
exactly
is the matter?
You
speak of
victory,
but
you
were not
happy,
did it
deceive
you?
It defeated you.

And everyone had to feel intense emotion on seeing those who returned from combat, and the brothers of those that had been killed the night before smile as evening fell, making signs and waving hello from one bank to another, like at a ferry that arrives in port, you wave your arms, you don't know anyone but you welcome them or wish the departing bon voyage, a good crossing. There were people on the bridge also, some leaning over sang. Natalina hurt her neck keeping her head back to stare at the inaccessible darkness. Because it was totally night now. She was happy to be there, she too.

She lowered her head and started to look at her red shoes and toes, and the tar on the edge of the wharf to this area that had burst under the heat and let several tips of grass break through. Her neighbors' feet. Sweating she was happy to have ran so much not to miss anything. She always adored fireworks.

I understand,
you
love her.
A black horse, a
white horse,
escaped and
spurting
high on the
mountain,
it's clear,
nonetheless,
no?

With cries of very young children and car-horns of newlyweds, we scampered up roofs of the cars parked on the side to see better, …a flaming arrow suddenly rose whistling, it burst high above and a bubbling spray illumined the sky then went out all at once meowing above heads of hair and ahhhhhhs and ohhhhhhhs.

Again! A second red and green spray exploded almost in the same place as the first one. A man took his son on his shoulders and Natalina immediately could no longer see anything. But this one was everywhere, it crackled, burned a hole in the air, this was one of the most beautiful pictures, cascades so long awaited, each full of gold, crammed with light, tumbling over and over again in the river water.

horse
sits
in the meadow, it
suffocates flies,
the other
follows and
rolls
up to
him
high on the
mountain
the two
thrilling, roll
on the carpet
flying as far as
Persia
because they are
princess and
prince

who knows?
you understand
now?

It was imposing for a such a little town, what taxes would have to pay for it! The balls of fire rolled in the night, spraying all the people gathered, the air smelled so strongly of power that you wanted to sneeze, to keep the good strong scent in your handkerchief.
The crowd stamped their feet and laughed. The fanfare passed, at least forty brass instruments sputtering. Natalina twisted her hands with happiness and suddenly thought of Daniel whom she'd left drinking his beer with small sips, his mouth his eyes full of foam behind the music, singing and dancing with the others on the other side of the bridge.

Battle
over,
it's
victory,
ravishing
petticoats,
mistakes
the pianist
at the ball

in his honor
Your Honor
Heros
rest,
take a fresh breath of joy,
do not have
a black soul,
are always hungry,
hungry

The applause lived up to the level of the spectacle. The small boat went by four times again with its spinning fires which lit up the waves, then there was the final, indescribable bouquet. We roasted lambs, afterwards, on the two riverbanks, and on the bridge they let all the billy goats go as far as the villages. The souls of the oldest apes stayed up and watched.
The men reunited under the six-peg tents, one woman standing waited on the road so that bus would bring her back home at the other end.
The night was short for many.

There is victory, there is the morning bird, oh, snatch muscle from sky, rubber bands, weight of figs spurts, rustling sky,

another plane makes a shadow between sun and house, noon, that and cloud sudden cloud invade the body of a traveler from the mountain above the sea, what an extraordinary view on the isles

Opens his bag and drinks from a bottle, there are leaves that lift again from the wind, just across Montecristu, a thoughtful Hero goes back down, twists his feet, not angel not grape thief, tired

End of the parade, end of day, dog curls up on the edge of the path,
dog dreams away

*Would you recognize this one, Lord-silent-violet, in the stream the mud
sticks, the herd passes sinking up to their horns the heart, doesn't leap anymore,
would you Recognize?*

*Don't fear ————— don't forget, as much as one fern or wave
trembling on its crest,*

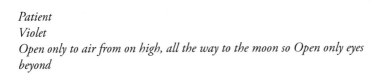

Patient
Violet
Open only to air from on high, all the way to the moon so Open only eyes
beyond

"laugh at the first one up" in red on the wall no longer
worn away—from tears and waves, salt of one or the Other great
among elders who Wish

Fly climbs the window pane, thus, sea descends again pebbles die down
a moment,

thus battle for a moment , Then all starts when this dies,
then this dies, and starts, victory approaches wolf's teeth growing longer
in the baskets,

victory the soft skin shredded, what splendor, from stars so high, and
ribbons, if you dance and sing, who knows, it may rain, the earth
needs it,

they cut reeds on the shore, (they failed to fall looking for them) they
cut, they make flutes and strokes everywhere such that they could and
a diving board, they jump pedaling each one behind the other waits his
turn,

Dust tolls on feet

Stones toll on feet Sun Tolls in the truck, at the feet of
isles sand tolls sea tolls one against the other again and again
sea lapping
lapping very far at this time

the truck shakes, a little groan from the crowd, undressed larva moans, it sings in the truck, this always happens and in a circle sometimes

Between sky and sand, there's me! there's me!
up to salt, dead water this time

Where is He with the valise, he spoke loud and thought loud, how he was hungry and thirsty! said the wicked wolf

and the cloud passed as clouds pass without looking, weighing
tons weighing nothing, on his shoulder a parrot a cotton ball a golden
saint, with curls

Where to go now, outside is inside I keep my slippers it's the
back of the garden, it rained, my basket filled with ceps and snails,
thanks to the following day!

He joined his fingers very properly, then lifted his hat in greeting, thanks

They were all heroes men and women, All women and all men in the truck that shook on the trail over there, they were there,

are here, will be, Tomorrow takes his crown of palm trees and drinks where he can and washes his plates in the basin, his fork, his knife, his glass with the dust from over there,

And wind which turns, there is a kind of house, because it's blurred, it's
dust and behind the crowd, their laughter and their pennies, a little doll
eats the flowers of her dress a shawl on her head, her chest Wood,
turns at the bottom of the basket, come back! There's a great deal of what and
come back!

Other trucks were there terrible iron-clad trucks, and the dying
crying will again be as sure as earth turns, Ditch will be jam-packed

Sends his ball that rolls to the edge of the grass and falls to the bottom,
another fishes it with a string, three boys taken by reverie, plunked on the edge

Much closer much closer much closer still, how, how and how,
to confuse, roll and twist swallow stay and shake keep crush find again
soft grass, swallow, Polyphemus's sizzling eye, eye that melts under
earth, turn yet turn within, Their carpenters' fingers

Their fingers today on buttons, his pigeon heart explodes, his
female, the women creak the pulleys, Ditch will be jam-packed, Ditch leaves
its teeth, bowl on bathroom sink

She has big black pants a white blouse which shines on the
boulevard, so She shines, always dances, is all ears, in
the hole, planted the diamond, planted the olive tree, planted the sun, the only frank
boy to arrive on time and who nibbles, and who laughs

Joy I want Joy, promise

It's bread, this winter day sun posed behind the curtain, who comes, it's She, constant companion, the bread the day the sun posed on her mouth and heart at the same instant mouth and heart,

Everyone knows it, Ditch, this hill —————— seen from the bottom

Everyone knows it, standing, whole arms, eyes facing, most, on nothing, *we must hand it over, we must hand it over, life has been given, life returned, life has been given, life returned*

The little house of zinc grows fainter, the driver croons, his Bessie (photo) posed on his knee, Hills still shine, plenty of room in the almost sorceress with her gloved fingers in the saloon

Who knows who we will become, and stupid me for centuries and centuries, everyone stupid for centuries and for a long time, I keep coming back, this is the homecoming, the favorite son, the purest and the most foolish among us

Here is the village, the well, it's me, I am old now I don't understand
if someone something nothing, otherwise a mule, turns around
collapses starts off again zigzagging disappears at the bend, tomorrow

So.

Let's kiss the world disappearing in the ditch swallowed and even
stars fall aside I hear the sleigh bells waxed swords bombed sparrows
dive also, lightning, ace of hearts, delicate ankles that have walked too
much, A kiss on the forehead, a kiss in the hands, a kiss on
the kiss

So, good-bye Hero, may those who follow be happy, oh, luck to everyone

Behind the window, look at the birds, winter cold, games, graves, games,

About the Author

Hélène Sanguinetti is also the author of *Domaine des englués, suivi de six réponses à Jean-Baptiste Para* (La Lettre Volée, 2017), *Et Voici La Chanson* (L'Amandier, 2012), *Alparegho, Pareil-à-rien* (Comp'Act, 2005), and reissued in 2015 by l'Amandier, *D'ici, de ce berceau* (Flammarion, 2003), and *De la main gauche, exploratrice* (Flammarion, 1999). Nominated for the prestigious Prix des Découvreurs, her work has received critical acclaim in *La Nouvelle Quinzaine Littéraire, L'Humanité, Le Monde, Le Figaro Littéraire,* and *Le Nouvel Observateur.* Poetry critic Claude Adelen praises Sanguinetti's poetry for "its emotional quality, physicality of verse, mythic intelligence and profound depth of being." Sanguinetti, also published in anthologies and online journals such as *Poezibao, Remue.Net, Terres de femmes,* and *Secousse,* participates in radio broadcasts, festivals, and interviews in France and abroad. Her work has been translated into Corsican, Finnish, Slovenian and Spanish; selections from *Domaine des englués,* translated into German, recently appeared in the bilingual anthology *Le Grand Huit/Die Achterbahn* (Wallstein Verlag/Le Castor Astral, 2018). Sanguinetti lives in Arles, France.

About the Translator

Ann Cefola's translations of Hélène Sanguinetti's work include *Alparegho, Like Nothing Else,* forthcoming from The Operating System's Unsilenced Texts series in 2019, *Hence this cradle* (Seismicity Editions, 2007), and poems in translation journals such as *eleven eleven, Exchanges, Inventory,* and *Transference.* Cefola is the recipient of a Witter Bynner Poetry Translation Residency and the Robert Penn Warren Award judged by John Ashbery. She is the author of *Free Ferry* (Upper Hand Press, 2017), and *Face Painting in the Dark* (Dos Madres Press, 2014); and the chapbooks *St. Agnes, Pink-Slipped* (Kattywompus Press, 2011), and *Sugaring* (Dancing Girl Press, 2007). Cefola lives and works in the New York suburbs. For more, see *www.anncefola.com* and *www.annogram.blogspot.com.*

ABOUT CHAX

Founded in 1984 in Tucson, Arizona, Chax has published more than 230 books in a variety of formats, including hand printed letterpress books and chapbooks, hybrid chapbooks, book arts editions, and trade paperback editions such as the book you are holding. From August 2014 until July 2018 Chax Press resided in Victoria, Texas, where it was located in the University of Houston-Victoria Center for the Arts. UHV has supported the publication of *The Hero*, which has also received support from friends of the press. Chax is a nonprofit 501(c)(3) organization which depends on support from various government private funders, and, primarily, from individual donors and readers.

In July 2018 Chax Press returned to Tucson, Arizona, while maintaining a partial affiliation with the University of Houston-Victoria. Our current address is 1517 North Wilmot Road no. 264, Tucson, Arizona 85712-4410.

Recent books include *A Mere Rica,* by Linh Dinh, *Visible Instruments,* by Michael Kelleher, *What's the Title?,* by Serge Gavronsky, *Diesel Hand,* by Nico Vassilakis, *At Night on The Sun,* by Will Alexander, *The Hindrances of Householders,* by Jennifer Barlett, *Who Do With Words,* by Tracie Morris, *Mantis,* by David Dowker, and *Rechelesse Pratticque,* by Karen Mac Cormack.

You may find CHAX at *https://chax.org/*